Deer, Moose, Elk & Caribou

Written by Deborah Hodge

Illustrated by Pat Stephens

KIDS CAN PRESS
WILDLIFE SERIES

Kids Can Press

For Dave, with love — DH
For Mike — PS

I would like to gratefully acknowledge the review of my manuscript by Barry Saunders, Registered Professional Biologist, wildlife consultant and former biologist with the British Columbia Ministry of Environment, Lands and Parks.

I would also like to thank my editor, Valerie Wyatt; my publishers, Ricky Englander and Valerie Hussey; and the entire team at Kids Can Press. It is a pleasure to work with you all.

Special thanks to Pat Stephens for her beautiful illustrations and to Marie Bartholomew for her lovely design of this series.

Kids Can Press acknowledges the financial support of the Ontario Arts Council, the Canada Council for the Arts and the Government of Canada, through the CBF, for our publishing activity.

Published in Canada by
Kids Can Press Ltd.
25 Dockside Drive
Toronto, ON M5A 0B5

Published in the U.S. by
Kids Can Press Ltd.
2250 Military Road
Tonawanda, NY 14150

www.kidscanpress.com

Edited by Valerie Wyatt
Designed by Marie Bartholomew

The hardcover edition of this book is smyth sewn casebound.
The paperback edition of this book is limp sewn with a drawn-on cover.
Manufactured in Shenzhen, China, in 2/2013 by C & C Offset.

CM 98 0 9 8 7 6 5 4 3 2
CM PA 98 0 9 8 7

Library and Archives Canada Cataloguing in Publication

Hodge, Deborah
    Deer, moose, elk and caribou

(Kids Can Press wildlife series)
Includes index.

ISBN 978-1-55074-435-4 (bound)
ISBN 978-1-55074-667-9 (pbk.)

1. Deer – Juvenile literature. 2. Moose – Juvenile literature. 3. Elk – Juvenile literature. 4. Caribou – Juvenile literature. I. Stephens, Pat. II. Title. III. Series.

QL737.U55H62 1998   j599.65   C97-931622-7

Kids Can Press is a *Corus*™ Entertainment company

Contents

Deer are wild

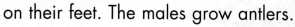

Deer are wild animals. They have big eyes, sharp hearing and a keen sense of smell. Deer depend on their senses to spot animals that are hunting them. Deer are always ready to run.

Deer, moose, elk and caribou are all members of the deer family. They all eat plants and have hooves on their feet. The males grow antlers.

Deer are mammals – furry, warm-blooded animals who breathe with lungs. Mammal babies drink their mothers' milk.

The moose is the largest deer in the
world. Its antlers can weigh as much as
an average 11-year-old child – about
40 kg (90 pounds).

Kinds of deer

There are five members of the deer family in North America: elk, moose, caribou, white-tailed deer and mule deer.

Elk (also known as wapiti) can be noisy. They grunt, squeal, whistle and roar. Females can weigh up to 300 kg (650 pounds). Males weigh up to 450 kg (1000 pounds).

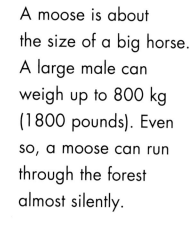

A moose is about the size of a big horse. A large male can weigh up to 800 kg (1800 pounds). Even so, a moose can run through the forest almost silently.

The mule deer has big ears, like a mule. It has a black-tipped tail and is sometimes called the black-tailed deer. Females weigh up to 72 kg (160 pounds). Large males can grow up to 215 kg (475 pounds).

The white-tailed deer flashes its tail as a warning signal to other deer. Full-grown adults weigh from 70 to 135 kg (150 to 300 pounds).

The caribou (also known as the reindeer) is the deer of the North. Its thick fur keeps it warm. Both male and most female caribou grow antlers. A female weighs up to 135 kg (300 pounds). Males can be twice as heavy.

Where deer live

Most members of the deer family live in wooded areas. Here they can find food and places to hide.

Moose live in forests or in swampy areas. They eat plants that grow in and around the water.

Caribou live in cold, northern areas, such as the Arctic tundra. They travel from place to place searching for food.

Most elk roam high in the mountains, where they can stay far away from people.

These white-tailed deer can easily hide in wooded areas.
The color of their fur blends in with the bushes and trees.

Why deer migrate

Some deer travel from place to place as the seasons change. This is called migrating.

In summer, elk and mule deer migrate up to lush mountain meadows. When snow falls, they travel back down to the valleys to find food.

Every spring, huge herds of caribou migrate to feeding grounds in the Far North. They cross icy lands and swollen rivers. Along the way, the females give birth. The babies can travel soon after birth. In fall, the caribou migrate back.

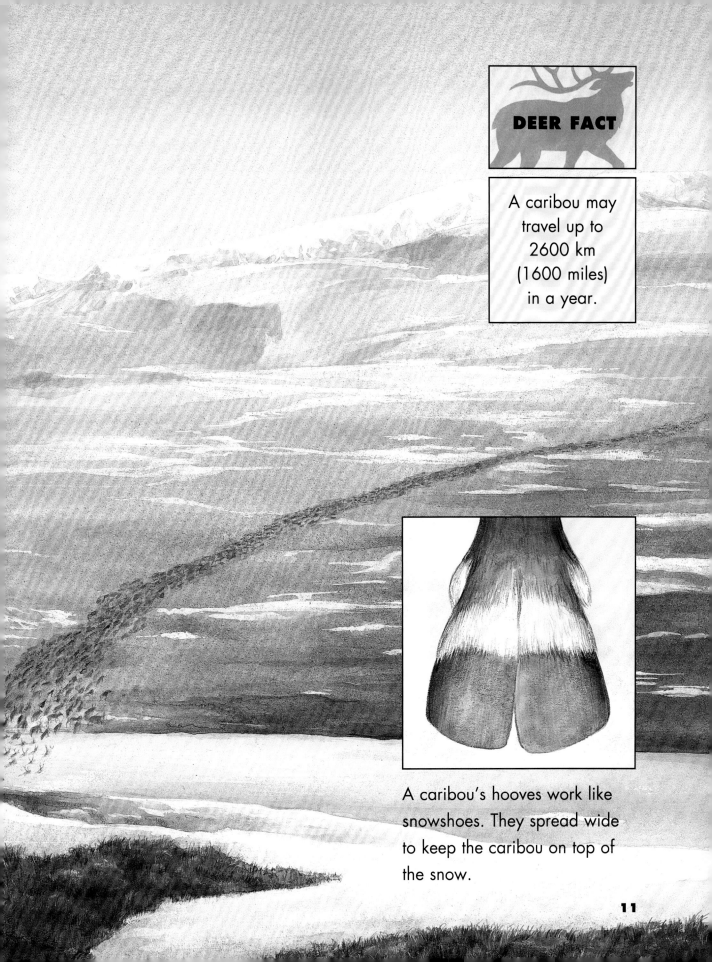

A caribou may travel up to 2600 km (1600 miles) in a year.

A caribou's hooves work like snowshoes. They spread wide to keep the caribou on top of the snow.

Deer food

All members of the deer family are plant eaters. In summer, they feed on grasses and green plants. In winter, they eat twigs, tree bark or mossy plants called lichens.

A deer is always on the alert for enemies, so it eats quickly. It nips off plants and swallows them almost whole. The food is stored in the deer's large stomach. When the deer is full, it lies down in a hidden spot. Here it can safely rest and digest its food.

Water plants are the moose's favorite summer food. A moose may dive deep down to find them. In a day, it eats as much as 90 big salad bowls of greens.

In winter, food is hard to find. Elk dig holes to find grasses and leaves under the snow.

Deer bodies

A deer's body is built to keep it safe from animals that hunt it.

Muscles

Thick muscles make the deer fast and strong.

Stomach

A deer's stomach has four parts. Food is stored in the largest part. When a deer is resting, it brings up bits of food. This "cud" is chewed into tiny pieces, then returned to the stomach to be digested.

Hooves

A deer runs swiftly on its tiptoes. Scent glands on the hooves let the deer leave signals for other deer.

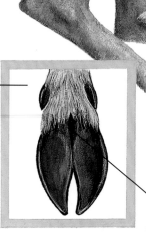

Scent gland

Antlers
All male deer (and most female caribou) grow and shed a set of antlers each year. Each set is larger than the one before. A deer uses its antlers to protect itself and to attract a mate.

Ears
Sharp hearing lets a deer know when danger is near.

Nose
A keen sense of smell tells the deer where enemies are hiding.

Eyes
Big eyes on the sides of the head let the deer see all around.

Bones
A deer's bones are light yet sturdy. Long legs help the deer run fast and jump high. In a single leap, a deer can spring over a 2.5 m (8 foot) fence.

How deer move

All members of the deer family are fast runners and strong swimmers. This helps them escape from enemies. When frightened, they race through the trees. Their long legs help them leap over big rocks and fallen trees.

Mule deer are sometimes called "jumpers" because they hop with stiff legs. Like a rabbit, the mule deer pushes off the ground with all four feet at the same time.

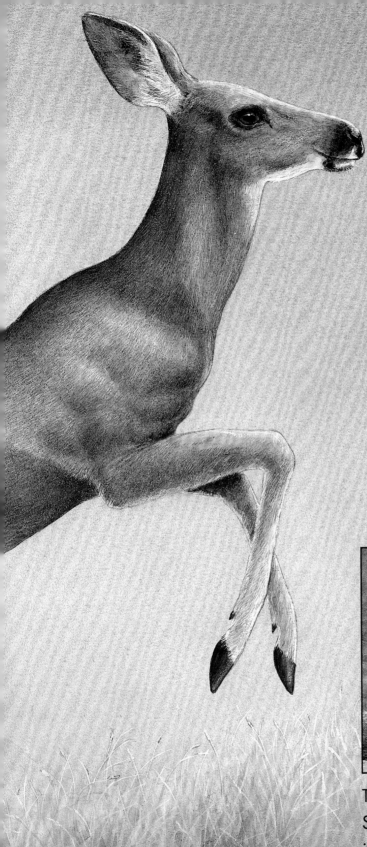

The caribou is a powerful swimmer.
Strong muscles and big hooves help
it pull through the water.

How deer live

Elk and caribou live in groups called herds. Living in a herd helps them stay safe from enemies.

Moose and white-tailed deer live alone for much of the year. But like other deer, they look for mates in the fall.

At mating time, the male deer marks off an area with urine. It rubs scent from its antlers on trees and bushes. Male elk call out to females with loud bugles and roars. Female moose bellow to the males.

This moose is shedding the velvet that carried blood to his antlers. After mating, he will shed the antlers too.

Deer shed their antlers in the spring. They grow a new set over the summer.

Male deer, such as these elk, battle with their sharp antlers. The strongest male will mate with the females.

How deer are born

A mother deer gives birth to one or two babies in late spring. Most babies are born in hidden bushy areas.

Within minutes, the baby takes its first wobbly steps. The mother may lead it to a new hiding spot. Here the baby will stay alone for up to two weeks. It has almost no scent, so it is safe from enemies – safer than it would be with its mother. From a distance, the mother watches for danger. She comes back to feed her baby often.

A baby white-tailed deer is called a fawn. Its spots help it stay hidden.

How deer grow and learn

A newborn deer feeds on its mother's milk. Her rich milk helps it to grow quickly. When it is a few weeks old, the baby begins to follow its mother. It copies her by nibbling on plants and grasses. The mother teaches her baby how to find food and stay safe.

A young deer is frisky and full of energy. It leaps, kicks, bucks and runs. Playing builds muscles and helps it learn how its body works.

By fall, the young deer is much bigger. Its spots are gone and new adult fur is growing in.

Baby moose are called calves. Like most young deer, they stay with their mother for one year. During this time, she will fiercely attack any enemy that comes near.

Less than a week after it is born, a baby deer can run faster than a human.

23

How deer protect themselves

The deer's main enemies are cougars and wolves. Other enemies include bears, coyotes, bobcats, lynx, wolverines and eagles. These hunters may not be fast enough to catch an adult deer, but baby deer are in great danger.

Most deer protect themselves by staying still and hiding. When frightened, they run. Their hooves leave large amounts of scent behind. The scent warns other deer of danger.

It is easier to keep safe in a herd. If one caribou senses danger, the whole herd gallops away in a great stampede. The movement confuses the wolves.

A frightened white-tailed deer stamps its feet. Other deer in the area hear the stamping and race away.

A single moose can fight off a pack of wolves. Its sharp hooves and huge antlers become deadly weapons.

Deer and people

For many years, native peoples depended on deer for food and clothing. They did not hunt more animals than they could use. But when European settlers arrived, they hunted great numbers of deer. Some, such as the elk, almost disappeared. Today, there are laws to protect the deer family.

To survive, the deer family needs wild, wooded areas. When people clear land for houses and roads, wild areas get smaller. The number of cougars and wolves also shrinks. With fewer enemies, too many deer end up in one area. Food becomes scarce, and some deer die. Others eat farmers' crops to stay alive.

All deer need food, water and space to roam. This mule deer fawn grows strong and healthy in the wild.

Deer around the world

There are about 40 species of deer in the world. They are mainly found in North and South America, Europe and Asia.

Deer are not naturally found in other continents of the world. But some have been taken to places such as Australia, New Zealand, North Africa and Antarctica. Now small numbers of deer live in these places.

Europe and Asia

Roe deer

Sika deer

Fallow deer

Asia

Musk deer

North America

Europe

Asia

Africa

South America

Australia

Chital

Muntjac

South America

Red brocket

Marsh deer

Pudu deer

Deer signs

Moose

White-tailed deer
and mule deer

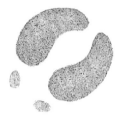

Caribou

Tracks
The big footprints on page 31 are the size of real moose
prints.

Elk

Scat
Scat is the name for deer droppings, or body waste.
Scientists know where a deer is by tracking its scat. This
scat looks like pellets. It shows that the elk was eating
shrubs and twigs.

Rubbing trees
Male deer rub their antlers on trees.
This helps them shed their velvet.

Words to know

calf: a baby moose, elk or caribou

fawn: a baby white-tailed deer or mule deer

herd: a group of deer that lives and travels together

lichens: mossy plants that grow on rocks and trees. Lichens are a favorite food of caribou.

mammal: a warm-blooded animal with hair covering, whose babies are born live and fed mother's milk

mating time: a time when a male and female deer come together to produce baby deer

migrate: to travel from place to place as the seasons change

resting spot: a hidden spot where a deer can safely rest and sleep

tundra: large, flat, treeless areas in the Arctic

velvet: soft fur that covers a deer's antlers and carries blood to them as they grow. Velvet is shed once the antlers are fully grown.

warm-blooded: having a warm body temperature, even when it is cold outside

Index